The Standard
PATTERN GLASS PRICE GUIDE

by Mollie Helen McCain

COLLECTOR BOOKS

P.O. Box 3009
Paducah, KY 42001

The current values in this book should be used only as a guide. They are not intended to set prices, which vary from one section of the country to another. Auction prices as well as dealer prices vary greatly and are affected by condition as well as demand. Neither the Author nor the Publisher assumes responsibility for any losses that might be incurred as a result of consulting this guide.

Additional copies of this book may be ordered from:

COLLECTOR BOOKS
P.O. Box 3009
Paducah, Kentucky 42001
@$5.95 Add $1.00 for postage and handling.

Copyright: Mollie Helen McCain, 1980
ISBN: 0-89145-155-2

Printed by IMAGE GRAPHICS, Paducah, Kentucky

Introduction

The names of patterns in this guide are from nomenclature used in *PATTERN GLASS PRIMER, A Pattern Guide to Early American Pressed Glass.* All patterns listed here are illustrated in the *PATTERN GLASS PRIMER.* A list of secondary pattern names is included at the end of the alphabetical pattern list of this price guide.

The prices listed in this guide are retail prices arranged in keys. Ranges and overlaps compensate for variations caused by geographical availability, dealer judgment, type of sale, etc.

Generally speaking, you will be paying a fair retail price if you use these keys; but if you are selling to a dealer your price should be somewhat lower.

Damaged pieces have less value than shown here. The wise buyer will not buy chipped or cracked pressed glass.

Tiny usage lines or minor folds or bubbles in the glass itself are not considered flaws that affect the price of the pattern.

These keys reflect prices of clear, crystal glass. *Colored glass* will command much higher prices in many instances.

Frequently heard are dire warnings about the abundance of *reproductions* and the caution that must be exercised. Reproductions are often easy to detect, however; and a little experience should make it safe to

47120

buy. Look for a wrinkled or mottled effect on clear portions of the pattern — an old pattern will be beautifully clear on these parts. Reproductions are frequently sloppy, with hobnails pointing unevenly; features in patterns blurred; lack of detail; etc. The glass may look dull; it will lack that smooth feel of old glass. Sometimes you will hear a dull thud instead of a bell-tone when the piece is tapped, although not all old glass rings. Tiny scratch and "scrub" lines are often visible on the bases of old glass which usually do not detract from prices.

Sugar Shakers (muffineers) were not made in abundance and command brisk prices. *Spill holders* are also not too common, and are generally found in older patterns. A lamp and spill set will bring premium prices.

Bowls can vary greatly in price because of size. Small berry bowls will be priced in lower portion of keys; large bowls in the upper bracket. Very large punch bowls may be priced in the next higher key.

Prices of *compotes* depend on several factors. A low-standard open compote will be priced in the lower bracket of the key; high-standard covered compotes in the higher bracket. Figural standards or lid knobs may push prices into the next key.

Plates are hard to price because of variations in size, with or without handles, special additional motifs, etc. Portrait plates in a given pattern may greatly accelerate price.

Butter dishes and *sugar bowls* carry prices in the lower range when they are open (no lids); covers increase their prices, and fancy or figural knobs on the covers increase their value even further.

Sauce dishes prices are meant to represent small, footed or non-footed dishes. A set of sauces may be priced lower than the key for a number of individual pieces.

Price Guide

	Key A	Key B	Key C	Key D	Key E	Key F
Bowl	$ 8.-12.	$12.-25.	$25.-40.	$35.-50.	$45.-60.	$60.+
Butter Dish	$14.-23	$20.-35.	$32.-45.	$45.-65.	$65.-95.	$95.-165.+
Cake Stand	$18.-25.	$25.-35.	$35.-50.	$50.-80.	$80.-120.	120.+
Celery	$11.-18.	$18.-30.	$30.-40.	$40.-70.	$60.-90.	$90.+
Compote	$17.-35.	$25.-40.	$35.-55.	$50.-80.	$75.-150.	$120.-200.+
Cordial	$ 6.-10.	$10.-20.	$20.-30.	$30.-45.	$45.-70.	$70.+
Creamer	$12.-25.	20.-35.	$25.-50.	$50.-65.	$65.-100.	$100.-165.+
Cruet	$ 8.-12.	$12.-20.	$18.-35.	$30.-50.	$40.-80.	$80.+
Decanter	$20.-30.	$30.-45.	$45.-60.	$60.-75.	$75.-100.	$100.-160.+
Egg Cup	$ 7.-13.	$13.-20.	$20.-30.	$30.-40.	$40.-50.	$50.+
Goblet	$ 9.-15.	$15.-22.	$23.-42.	$43.-65.	$50.-85.	$85.+
Jam Jar, Covered	$12.-18.	$15.-30.	$25.-50.	$45.-65.	$65-100.	$100.+
Mug	$10.-15.	$16.-22.	$22.-35.	$35.-50.	$50.-65.	$65.+
Pitcher, Water or Milk	$20.-35.	$30.-50.	$40.-70.	$70.-110.	$110.-150.	$150.-200.+
Plate	$10.-15.	$12.-20.	$20.-30.	$31.-50.	$50.-60.	$60.+
Relish Dish	$ 6.-10.	$11.-15.	$16.-22.	$22.-40.	$40.-50.	$50.+
Salt, Master	$ 1.-15.	$10.-20.	$20.-30.	$26.-35.	$35.+	
Salt Shaker	$ 7.-12.	$10.-14.	$12.-25.	$25.-40.	$30.-60.	$60.+
Sauce Dish	$ 3.- 8.	$ 6.-12.	$10.-20.	$18.-24.	$25.+	
Spill Holder	$20.-40.	$25.-45.	$35.-50.	$40.-55.	$45.-60.	$60.+
Spoon Holder	$8.-15.	$12.-18.	$15.-30.	$25.-45.	$40.-65.	65.-100.
Sugar Bowl	$12.-25.	$20.-40.	$35.-55.	$50.-80.	$70.-100.	$100.+
Sugar Shaker	$15.-22.	$20.-35.	$30.-50.	$45.-60.	$60.+	
Syrup*	$12.-20.	$18.-35.	$28.-42.	$35.-70.	$70.+	
Toothpick	$ 6.-14.	$15.-23.	$20.-30.	$30.-40.	$40.-50.	$50.+
Tumbler	$ 6.-12.	$10.-25.	$18.-30.	$25.-40.	$40.+	
Waste Jar	$ 8.-12.	$10.-25.	$20.-40.	$30.-50.	$50.+	
Wine	$ 6.-12.	$10.-22.	$20.-40.	$40.-50.	$50.+	

*Original Top on Syrup is not too important to pricing.

Pattern	Key	
Acanthus Leaf	E	(Slag)
Acanthus Scroll	A	
Acorn	C	
Acorn, Beaumont's	B	
Acorn Band	C	
Acorn Diamonds	A	
Actress	D	
Actress Chain	D	
Ada	B	
Adams Diamond	C	
Adams Saxon	A	
Adams #329	A	
Admiral	B	
Admiral Dewey	D	
Aegis	D	
Aetna	A	
Aetna #300	B	
Aida	D	
Alabama	A	
Alba Blossoms	C	Opaque glass
Albany	B	
Albion	D	
All Over Diamond	B	
Almond Thumbprint	C	
Amazon	A	
Amboy	B	
American Beauty	A	
Angelus	A	
Anglesey	A	
Angora	A	
Angular	A	
Anthemion	B	
Antwerp	A	
Apple & Grape in Scroll	C	

Actress Chain

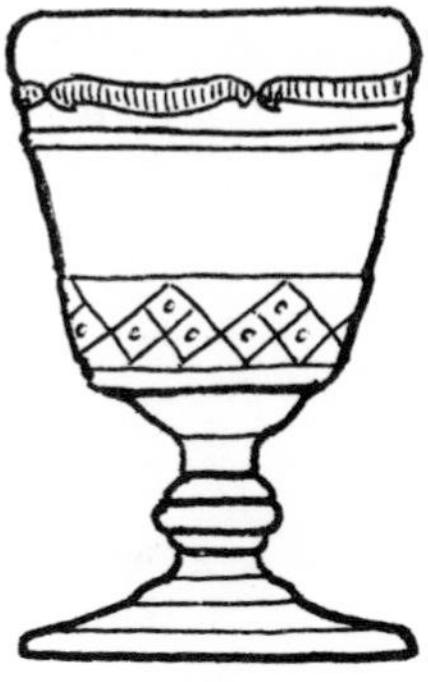

Angora

7

Pattern	Key
Apple Blossom	D..Milk Glass
Apollo	C
Aquarium	E
Arabesque	B
Arabian	A
Arch & Forget-Me-Not Bands	B
Arch & Sunburst	B
Archaic Gothic	B
Arched Cane & Fan	B
Arched Diamond Points (Massachusetts)	B
Arched Fleur-De-Lis	B
Arched Grape	B
Arched Leaf	B
Arched Ovals	A
Arched Panel	A
Arched Tripod	D . . With stem
Argonaut Shell	C . . Colored Key E+
Argus	C . . Flint pitcher Key F
Arizona (Tepee)	B
Arrowhead	B
Arrowhead in Oval	B
Arrowsheaf	B
Art	C
Art Nouveau	A
Ashburton	D
Ashland	A
Aster & Leaf	B
Atlanta	B
Atlas	D
Atlas Square	B
Aurora	B
Avocado	A . . "Depression glass"
Avon	C
Aztec	A

Massachusetts

Aster & Leaf

*Flint — Key D

Bakewell Block

Bar and Diamond

Pattern	Key
Barrel Excelsior	D
Barrelled Thumbprint	B
Bars & Buttons	B
Basket Weave	A
Basket Weave with Cable	A
Basket Weave with Frosted Leaf	A
Beacon Light	A
Bead & Bar Medallion	B
Bead & Chain	A
Bead & Loop	A
Bead & Panel	A
Bead & Scroll	A
Bead Column	A
Bead Swag	B
Beaded Acanthus	B
Beaded Acorn	B
Beaded Arch Panels	B
Beaded Band	B
Beaded Band & Panel	A
Beaded Block	B
Beaded Block, Imperial's	A
Beaded Bottom	C
Beaded Bulb	A
Beaded Bull's-Eye & Drape (Alabama)	A
Beaded Chain	B
Beaded Circle	B
Beaded Coarse Bars	A
Beaded Dart Band	B
Beaded Dewdrop	C
Beaded Diamond	A
Beaded Diamond Band	B
Beaded Ellipse	A
Beaded Ellipse & Fan	B
Beaded Fan	B
Beaded Fine Cut	A

Bead & Chain

Bead Swag

. . Flint Key C

. . Cov. butter Key E

10

Pattern	Key
Beaded Flower	A
Beaded Grape	C
Beaded Grape Medallion	C
Beaded Lobe	B
Beaded Loops	C
Beaded Medallion	C
Beaded Oval	A
Beaded Oval & Scroll	A
Beaded Oval Band	B
Beaded Ovals in Sand	B
Beaded Panels	A
Beaded Raindrop	B
Beaded Rib	A
Beaded Rope Panel	A
Beaded Swirl	A
Beaded Swirl & Disc	B
Beaded Thumbprint Block	B
Beaded Triangle	A
Beaded Tulip	C
Beaded Yoke (Bead Swag)	B
Beads & Bark	C . . Slag only
Bearded Head	C
Beatty Honeycomb	B
Beatty Rib	C
Beatty #106 (Spiralled Triangle)	B
Beaumont's Columbia	B
Beautiful Lady	B
Beauty	A
Beaver Band	D
Bedford, The	B
Belfast	B
Bellaire Basketweave	C
Bellaire One	C
Bellaire Two	A
Bell & Pins	B
Belle	A

Bellaire One

Bellaire Two

11

Pattern	Key	
Bellflower	E	
Belmont Diamond	B	
Belmont's Reflecting Fans	B	
Belmont's Royal	B	
Belted Icicle	A	
Belted Panel	B	
Berlin	B	
Berry Cluster	C	With perfect berry
Bethlehem Star	B	
Bevelled Diagonal Block	A	
Bevelled Diamond & Star	B	
Bevelled Star	B	
Bicycle Girl	F	
Big Button	B	
Big Diamond	C	
Big Horseshoe	A	
Big Star	A	
Big X	A	
Bigler	C	Handled whiskey (see Mug) Key E
Biliken Flute	C	
Bird Salt		(See Salt Shaker) Key D
Bird & Strawberry	C	
Bird & Tree	D	
Bird Handled	C	
Bird in Ring	C	
Bismarc Star	C	
Blackberry	B	
Blackberry Band	B	
Blaze	C	Flint Key D
Blazing Cornucopia	B	
Bleeding Heart	C	
Block	A	
Block & Bar	C	
Block & Circle	A	
Block & Dent	B	
Block & Double Bar	A	

Berlin

Bevelled Diamond & Star

Block & Double Bar

Pattern	Key

Block & Fan . . . . B
Block & Honeycomb . . . . B
Block & Palm . . . . A
Block & Panel . . . . A
Block & Pillar . . . . A
Block & Pleat . . . . A
Block & Rib . . . . A
Block & Sunburst . . . . A
Block & Triple Bars . . . . B
Block Band, Squares . . . . A
Block Band, Diamond . . . . B
Block with Stars . . . . B
Block on Stilts C
Block with Thumbprint . . . . B
Block with Thumbprint,
   Late . . . . B
Blocked Arches . . . . A
Blocked Thumbprint . . . . E
Blocked Thumbprint Band . . . . A
Blossom . . . . B
Blown Swirl . . . . B
Blue Heron C
Bohemian . . . . B
Boling . . . . B
Bontec . . . . A
Boot C
Boot on Fan . . . . B
Bordered Ellipse . . . . B
Bosc Pear . . . . B
Boston . . . . A
Bouquet . . . . B
Bowline . . . . A
Bow Tie . . . . B
Box Pleat . . . . B
Boxed Star . . . . A
Bradford Grape . . . . D
Branched Tree . . . . B
Brazen Shield . . . . A
Brickwork . . . . A

Block Band — Squares

Block Band — Diamond

Pattern	Key
Bridal Rosettes	B
Brilliant	B
Bringing Home the Cows	F
Brittanic	B
Broken Bands	A
Broken Bar & Thumbprint	B
Broken Column	C
Brooch Band	A
Brooklyn	D
Bryce	C
Buckingham	B
Buckle (Flint-Key D)	B
Buckle & Diamond	B
Buckle & Shield	B
Buckle with English Hobnail	B
Buckle with Star	C
Budded Ivy	B
Bulbous Base	B
Bulging Corn	B
Bullet Emblem	F
Bull's-Eye (Non-flint Key B)	D
Bull's-Eye & Bar (Flint Key E; Egg cup F)	D
Bull's-Eye & Broken Column	E
Bull's-Eye & Buttons	B
Bull's-Eye & Daisy (Flint Key D)	B
Bull's-Eye & Fan	A
Bull's-Eye & Loop	D
Bull's-Eye & Prism	D
Bull's-Eye & Rosette	C
Bull's-Eye & Wishbone	C
Bull's-Eye Band	D
Bull's-Eye in Heart (Heart with Thumbprint)	C
Bull's-Eye with Diamond-Points	F
Bull's-Eye with Fleur-De-Lis*	D
Bull's-Eye Variant (Texas Bull's-Eye)	B
Butterfly	B
Butterfly Ears (Mustard - see sugar bowl)	A

*Pitcher, celery, butter — Key E

Pattern	Key
Butterfly Handles	B
Butterfly with Spray	D
Button & Button	B
Button & Star	A
Button & Star Panel	B
Button Arches	B
Button Band	B
Button Block	B
Button Panel	B
Buttressed Arch	A
Buttressed Loop	B
Buttressed Sunburst	A
Buzz Star	A

Cane & Rosette

Pattern	Key
Cabbage Leaf	D
Cabbage Rose	C
Cable	D
Cable Variant	D
Cable with Ring	D
Cactus	C
Cadmus	A
California (Beaded Grape)	C
Cambridge Colonial	A
Canadian	C
Cane	A
Cane & Cable	A
Cane & Fan	A
Cane & Rosette	B
Cane Column	A
Cane Horseshoe	B
Cane Medallion	B
Cane Pinwheel	A
Cane Shield	A
Cannonball	B
Cannonball Pinwheel	A
Canton House	C

Cannonball

Pattern	Key
Cape Cod	C
Capstan	A
Cardinal Bird	C
Carltec	A
Carmen	B
Carnation	A
Carolina	C
Cartridge Belt	A
Casco	B
Cathedral	B
Cat's-Eye	B
Cat's-Eye & Fan	B
Cattail & Waterlily	B
Cavitt	B
Celtic	A
Celtic Cross	B
Centennial 1876	D
Centennial Shield	D
Centipede	A
Central #438	A
Central #520	A
Central #560	A
Central #1879	A
Ceres	C
Chain & Shield	A
Chain & Swag	D . . (Milk Glass)
Chain, Early	B
Chain, Ft. Pitt	B
Chain Thumbprints	A
Chain with Star	B
Chalice	C . . (Milk Glass)
Challinor #304	A
Challinor #309	A
Challinor #313	B
Challinor #314	B
Chandelier	C
Chastity	A
Checkerboard	B
Checkerboard Band	B
Checker with Rib Band	A

Cathedral

Chandelier

Pattern	Key	
Checkers	A	
Chelsea	A	
Cherry & Cable	B	
Cherry	B	
Cherry & Fig	B	
Cherry Lattice	B	
Cherry Sprig	B	
Cherry with Thumbprint	B	
Chestnut Oak	C	
Chick	B	
Chilson (Flint)	F	
Chippendale	A	
Chrysanthemum Sprig	E	Custard; rare in blue
Church Windows	A	
Circle X	A	
Circled Scroll	B	
Circular Saw	A	
Clark	B	
Classic	E	
Classic Medallion	B	
Clear Diagonal Band	A	
Clear Lion Head	C	
Clear Ribbon	C	
Clear Ribbon Variant	B	
Clear Stork	C	
Clematis	B	
Climax	A	
Clio	A	
Clover	A	
Coarse Cut & Block	A	
Coarse Zig-Zag	B	
Coat-of-Arms	B	
Coin & Dewdrop	C	
Coin, Columbian	D	
Coin, U.S.	F	
Collins	B	
Colonial	C	
Colonial & Mitre	A	"Depression Glass"
Colonial Fluted	A	
Colonial Panel	A	

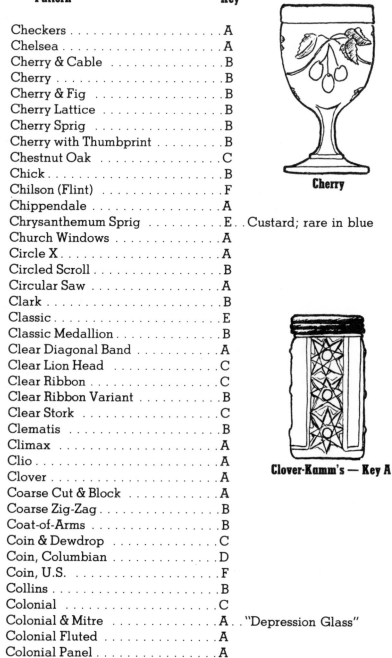

Cherry

Clover-Kamm's — Key A

17

Pattern	Key
Colonial with Diamond Band	B
Colonial with Garland	B
Colonis	A
Colorado	C
Colossus (Lacy Spiral)	C
Columbia	B
Columbia, Federal	A . . "Depression Glass"
Column Block	B
Columned Thumbprints	B
Compact	B
Concaved Almond	B
Concaved Arrowheads	B
Connecticut	C
Connecticut Flute	A
Continental	C
Conventional Band	B
Coolidge Drape	(Lamp see decanter Key D)
Co-op Block	A
Co-op Columbia	A
Co-op #190	A
Co-op #323	A
Co-op #1908	A
Co-op's Royal	A
Coral Gables	B
Cord & Bars	A
Cord & Tassel	C
Cord Drapery	C . . Butter Key D
Cordova	B
Cornell	A
Corn	B
Corn Sphere	B
Corn with Husk	C
Cornucopia	B
Corona (Sunk Honeycomb)	B
Corrigan	C
Corset with Thumbprint	A
Cosmos	F . . Milk Glass; Lamp (See Butter)
Cottage	B
Cradled Prisms	A

Colonis

Colorado

Concaved Almond

Corrigan

18

Pattern	Key	
Cranesbill	A	
Crazy Patch	B	
Creased Hexagon Block	B	
Crisscross Band	A	
Crochet Band	A	
Crocus	B	Milk Glass
Croesus	C	
Cross Bands	B	
Crossbar	A	
Crossbar & Cane	A	
Crossbar Handle	A	
Crossed Block	B	
Crossed Discs	A	
Crossed Shield	B	
Cross in Diamond	B	
Crown	A	
Crowfoot (Yale)	B	
Crystal	A	
Crystal Queen	A	
Crystal Rock	A	
Crystal Wedding	D	
Crystalina	A	
Cube	A	
Cube & Diamond	B	
Cube, Late	A	"Depression Glass"
Cube with Fan	A	
Cupid & Venus	D	
Curled Leaf	B	
Currant	B	
Currier & Ives	C	
Curtain	B	
Curtain & Block	A	
Curtain Tie-Back	B	
Cut Block	B	
Cut Log	C	
Cuttlebone	B	
Cyclone	B	
Czarina	A	
Czarina with Fan	A	
Dagger	A	
Dahlia	C	

Crown

Currier & Ives

19

Dahlia & Leaf . . . . B
Daisy — "Depression Glass" . . . . A
Daisy & Button (Shoe - See Decanter) . . . . B
Daisy & Button Band . . . . B
Daisy & Button Oval Medallion . . . . B
Daisy & Button "V" . . . . B
Daisy & Button Variant . . . . A
Daisy & Button with Crossbar . . . . B*
Daisy & Button with Crossbar, Pointed . . . . B
Daisy & Button with Narcissus . . . . B
Daisy & Button with Prisms . . . . B
Daisy & Button with Thumbprint . . . . B
Daisy & Palm . . . . B
Daisy & Scroll . . . . A
Daisy Band . . . . B
Daisy in Diamond . . . . B
Daisy in Oval . . . . A
Daisy-in-Square . . . . A
Daisy Medallion . . . . A
Daisy Whorl . . . . B
Dakota C
Dancing Goat . . . . D
Dart . . . . A
Deep Star . . . . A
Deer Alert . . . . E
Deer & Dog (Butter with dog — Key F) . . . . E
Deer & Oak Tree . . . . E
Deer & Pine Tree . . . . D
Deer with Lily-of-the-Valley . . . . D
Delaware . . . . B
Delos . . . . A
Delta . . . . A
Despot . . . . A
Dew & Raindrop . . . . A
Dewberry . . . . B
Dewdrop . . . . A
Dewdrop & Star C
Dewdrop & Flowers . . . . B
Dewdrop in Points . . . . B
Dewdrop with Star C

*Cruet — Key E

Pattern	Key
Diagonal Band	A
Diagonal Band with Fan	B
Diagonal Bar Band	A
Diagonal Frosted Ribbon	B
Diamond & Long Sunburst	B
Diamond & Sunburst	A
Diamond & Sunburst, Early	A
Diamond & Sunburst Zippers	A
Diamond Band	A
Diamond Bar & Block	A
Diamond Block	A
Diamond Block with Fan	A
Diamond Crystal	A
Diamond Cut with Leaf	B
Diamond Fan	B
Diamond Flute	A
Diamond in Diamond	A
Diamond in Points	D
Diamond in Space	A
Diamond Lace	B
Diamond Lattice	A
Diamond Mirror	A
Diamond Point	E
Diamond Point & Punty	A
Diamond Point Discs	B
Diamond Point Loop	B
Diamond Point with Fan	A
Diamond Point with Panels	C
Diamond Prisms	A
Diamond Quilted	A
Diamond Quilted Imperial	A
Diamond Ridge	A
Diamond Rosettes	C
Diamond Side	A
Diamond Stem	A
Diamond Sunburst	B
Diamond Swag	B

Diamond Ridge

..Milk Glass Miniature

..Non-flint Key B

Diamond Swag

21

Pattern	Key
Diamond Swirl	B
Diamond Thumbprint	F
Diamond Waffle	A
Diamond Wall	A
Diamond Web	A
Diamond with Diamond Point	B
Diamond with Dual Fan	B
Diamonds & Dewdrops	B
Diamonds with Double Fans	A
Diapered Flower	D..Opaque Blue
Dice & Block	A
Dickenson	D
Dirago Pear	A
Disc & Fern	B
Dithridge #25	C..Milk Glass
Divided Block with Sunburst	A
Divided Diamonds	C
Divided Hearts	E
Dixie Belle	A
Dog Hunting	F
Doric & Pansy	A.."Depression glass"
Dot	C
Dot & Dash	A
Dotted Loop	A
Double Band Forget-Me-Not	B
Double Beaded Band	A
Double Beetle Band	B
Double Circle	A
Double Crossroads	A
Double Dahlia & Lens	B
Double Daisy	B..Compote Key E
Double Diamond Panels	B
Double Donut	C
Double Fan	A
Double Greek Key	C
Double Icicle	A
Double Line Swirl	B
Double Loop	B

Diamond Point Thumbprint
Key B

Double Daisy

22

Pattern	Key
Double Loop & Dart	A
Double Petalled Flute	A
Double Pinwheel	A
Double Rib	C . . Milk Glass
Double Ribbon	A
Double Scroll	A
Double Spear	B
Double Thumbprint Band	A
Double Zig-Zag	B
Doyle Comet	A
Doyle's Shell	A
Doyle's #11	A
Doyle's #76	A
Doyle's #80	A
Doyle's #400	B
Dragon	D
Draped Garland	B
Draped Jewel	C
Draped Window	F
Drapery	A
Drum	C
Duchess	B
Duncan	B
Duncan Block	A
Duncan Flute	A
Duncan Panel	B
Duncan #14	A
Duncan #16	A
Duncan #30	B
Duncan #37	A
Duncan #40	A
Duncan #42	B
Duncan #63	B
Duncan #71	A
Duncan #77	A
Duncan #904	A
Duncan #2001	A
Duncan & Miller #1	A
Duncan & Miller #6	A

Dragon

Drapery

Pattern	Key
Duncan & Miller #6	A
Duncan & Miller #8	A
Duncan & Miller #11	A
Duncan & Miller #13	A
Duncan & Miller #14	A
Duncan & Miller #16	A
Duncan & Miller #37	A
Duncan & Miller #46	A
Duncan & Miller #47	A
Duncan & Miller #69	A
Duncan & Miller #70	A
Duncan & Miller #76	A
Duncan & Miller #212	A
Duncan & Miller #313	A
Duncan's Late Block	A
Dutchess Flute (Flute)	C
Dutchess Loop	B
Eagle's Fleur-De-Lis	A
Early Panelled Grape Band	B
Ear of Corn	C
East Liverpool	B
Edgerton	A
Edgewood	A
Effulgent Star	C
Egg Band	C
Egg in Sand	C
Egyptian	D
Eight-O-Eight	B
Electric	B
Ellipse & Star	A
Ellipse One	A
Ellipse Two	A
Elmino	A
Elson's Block	A
Empire	A
Empress	A
Empress 2	A
English	A
English Cane	A

Ellipse One

Ellipse Two

Empress

Empress 2

24

Pattern	Key
English Colonial	B
English Hobnail	A
English Hobnail & Thumbprint	A
English Quilting	D
Enigma (Wyoming)	B
Essex	A
Esther	B
Etched Band	B
Etched Fern	C
Etched Grape	B
Etched Rectangle	B
Etruscan	C
Euclid	A
Eugenie	C
Eureka	C
Everglades	A
Excelsior, Early	C
Eye Band	A
Eyebrows	A
Eyelet	A
Eyewinker	D
Faceted Flower	B
Faceted Rosette Band	A
Fagot	D
Falling Leaves	A
Famous	A
Fan & Feather	A
Fan & Star	B
Fan Band	A
Fancy Arch	A
Fancy Cut	A
Fancy Diamonds	B
Fancy Fans	A
Fancy Loop	C- Toothpick Key E
Fandango	B
Fan with Crossbars	A
Fan with Diamond	A

Essex

Everglades

Fagot

25

Pattern	Key
Fan with Split Diamond	A
Fashion	A
Feather	B
Feather & Block	B
Feather Band	A
Feather Duster	B
Feathered Ovals	A
Feathered Points	A
Fern	A
Fern Garland	A
Fern Sprays	B
Ferris Wheel	A
Festoon	B
Festooned Stars	B
Fickle Block	A
File	B
Findlay #19	B
Fine Cut	B
Fine Cut & Block	C
Fine Cut & Diamond	B
Fine Cut & Panel	A
Fine Cut & Rib	A
Fine Cut Medallion	C
Fine Feather	A
Fine Rib	D
Fine Ribbed Anchor & Shield	D
Fish	A
Fishbone	A
Fishbone Bow	A
Fishnet & Poppies	C . Milk glass
Fishscale	B
Fishscale Swirl	B
Flamboyant	A
Flare Top Flute	C
Flat Diamond & Panel	F
Flat Diamond Box	B
Flat Iron	B
Flat Oval	B
Flat Panel	A

Fashion

Fine Cut Medallion

Fish

26

Pattern	Key	
Flat Panelled Star	A	
Flattened Diamond & Sunburst	B	
Flattened Fine Cut	B	
Flattened Hobnail	A	
Flattened Sawtooth	B	
Flat-to-Round Panel	A	
Flawless	A	
Fleur-De-Lis	B	
Fleur-De-Lis & Tassel	B	
Flickering Flame	A	Ruby-stained Key B; Syrup Key D
Flora	B	
Floral Diamond	A	
Floral & Diamond Band	A	"Depression glass"
Floral Oval	B	
Florida	B	
Florida Palm	B	
Florida Pineapple	B	
Flower & Bud	A	
Flower & Honeycomb	A	
Flower & Panel	B	
Flower & Pleat	A	
Flower & Quill	C	
Flower Band, Lee's	C	
Flower Band Barrel	B	
Flower Band, Warman's	C	Milk Glass
Flower Basket	B	
Flower Fan	A	
Flower Flange	D	
Flower Medallion	C	
Flower Pot	C	
Flower Windows	A	
Flower with Cane	B	
Flowered Oval	B	
Flowered Scroll	B	
Flute & Cane	A	
Flute & Crown	A	
Fluted Rib	A	
Fluted Ribbon	A	
Flute	C	

Flat Panelled Star

Flower Band, Lee's

Wild Rose with Scrolling

Pattern	Key
Fluted Scrolls	B
Flying Birds	C
Flying Stork	C
Flying Swan	B . . Slag — Key E
Foggy Bottom	B
Forget-Me-Not in Scroll	B
Formal Daisy	A
Fostoria Block	(Not EAPG)
Fostoria's Priscilla	B
Fostoria's Sterling	A
Fostoria's Swirl	B
Fostoria's Victoria	B
Fostoria's #551	A
Fostoria's #952	A
Fostoria's #956	A
Fostoria's #1008	C . . Milk Glass
Fostoria's #1119 (Sylvan)	A
Fostoria's #1231	A
Four Petal	D
Four Thumbprints	A
Fox & Crow	D
Framed Jewel	B
Framed Blocks	C
Franklin Flute	A
Fringed Drape	A
Frisco	B
Frost Crystal	A
Frosted Block	A
Frosted Circle	C
Frosted Eagle	C . . with eagle finial
Frosted Eagle Two	C . . with eagle finial
Frosted Leaf	E
Frosted Medallion	A
Frosted Ribbon	C

Foggy Bottom

Flower Band, Warman's

Pattern	Key
Frosted Ribbon — Double Bars	B
Frosted Stork	E
Fruit Band	B
Fulton	A
Funnel Rosette	B
Fuschia	A
Gaelic	A
Garden of Eden	C
Garfield Drape	C
Garland	B
Garland of Roses	A
Garter Band	A
Gathered Knot	A
Geneva	C . . Custard 150% higher
Georgia Belle	B
Giant's Bull's-Eye	D . . Non-flint Key B
Giant Flute	A
Giant Sawtooth	C
Gibson Girl	F
Giraffe	C
Globe & Star	B
Gooseberry	B
Gothic (Cathedral)	B
Gothic Windows	A
Grand	B
Grape & Cherry	D . . Milk Glass
Grape & Festoon	B
Grape & Festoon with Shield	B
Grape & Gothic Arches	A
Grape Band	B
Grape with Holly Band	B
Grape with Overlapping Foliage	B . . Non-Flint Key A
Grape with Scroll Medallion	A
Grape with Thumbprint	C

Fulton

Gibson Girl

Pattern	Key
Grape with Vine	B
Grape without Vine	A
Grasshopper with Insect	C . . Check wings of insect for damage
Grasshopper without Insect	B
Grated Arch	A
Grated Diamond & Sunburst	A
Grated Ribbon	B
Grecian	A
Greek Cross Band	A
Greek Key	C
Green Herringbone	B . . Green Key D
Greenburg's #130	B
Grogan	A
Gyro	A

Green Herringbone

Pattern	Key
Hairpin	C . . Flint
Hamilton	D . . Flint
Hamilton with Leaf	C . . Tumbler 2 to 3 X C
Hammond	C
Hand	C
Hand & Corn	E
Hand & Fishscale	E+
Hanging Basket	B
Hanging Leaf.................	C . . Milk Glass
Harmony	A
Harp	E . . Goblet rare
Hartford	A
Hartley	A
Harvard	B
Harvard Yard	A
Hawaiian Lei	B
Heart	E
Heart Band	C . . Ruby-Stained price

Pattern	Key
Heart Plume	B
Hearts & Arches	E+
Heart, Sandwich	E
Heart Stem	C
Heart with Thumbprint	B..Early Key C
Heavy Diamond	A
Heavy Drape	B
Heavy Fine Cut	B
Heavy Gothic	B
Heavy Jewel	B
Heavy Panelled Fine Cut	A
Heavy Rib	A
Heck	B

Heisey Patterns:

150	B
305	B
343	B
339-2	A
343½	B
357	B
379	A
1225	B

Heisey #357

Heisey's Chrysanthemum	B
Heisey's Coarse Ribbing	B
Heisey's Colonial	A
Heisey's Greek Key	B
Heisey's Panelled Cane	B
Heisey's Pineapple & Fan	B
Heisey's Sunburst	B
Helene	B
Hen on Nest	For price see Goblet Key A
Henrietta	B
Hercules Pillar	C
Hero	B
Heron	C
Herringbone	B
Herringbone Buttress	C
Herringbone Rib	B

31

Pattern	Key	
Hexagon Block	C	
Hexagon Bull's-Eye	B	
Hexagon Star	A	
Hexagonal Block Band	A	
Hickman	A	
Hidalgo	B	
High-Hob	A	
Hobbs Block	E	
Hobbs Diamond & Sunburst	B	
Hobnail	A	
Hobnail, Ball Foot	B	
Hobnail Band	A	
Hobnail in Big Diamonds	C	
Hobnail Pineapple	A	Barber bottle (See compote — Key C)
Hobnail with Thumbprint Base	A	
Hobnail with Fan	A	
Hob Star	A	
Holland	A	
Hollis	B	
Holly	E	
Holly Amber (Holly Clear)	E	If amber, 5 X Key E
Holly Band	D	
Home	B	
Homestead	B	with etched leaf
Honeycomb	B	
Honeycomb & Zipper	A	
Honeycomb Obi	B	
Honeycomb with Flower Rim	B	
Honeycomb with Star	B	
Hook	B	
Hooped Barrel	A	
Hops Band	B	
Horn of Plenty	D	
Horsehead Medallion	E	
Horseshoe	C	Master Salt 2 X C
Horseshoe Curve	A	
Hourglass	C	
Hovik	A	
Huber	C	
Hummingbird	C	

Hexagon Block

Hovik

Hungarian

Interlocked Hearts

Pattern	Key
Iona	A
I.O.U.	B
Iowa	C
Iron Kettle	A
Iris with Meander	B
Isis	A
Ivanhoe	B
Ivy in Snow	A
Ivy Spray	A
Jabot	B
Jacob's Coat	A
Jacob's Ladder	C
Jam Jar	A
Janssen	A
Japanese	C
Japanese Iris	C
Jasper	B
Jefferson Shell	B

Ivanhoe

Jefferson Patterns:

#1	A
#2	A
#250	A
#254 (The Jefferson)	A
#270	A
Jersey	C
Jersey S	E+ Very Early
Jersey Swirl	B
Jewel	B
Jewel & Festoon	A
Jewel & Flower	B
Jewelled Heart	B
Jewelled Moon & Star	B
Jewelled Rosettes	C
Jewel with Dewdrop (Kansas)	B
Job's Tears (Art)	C
Jubilee	A
Jumbo	E

Jewelled Heart

Pattern	Key	
Kayak	A	
Kentucky	B	
Keystone	C	
King's Crown	B	Ruby-stained — Key C
King's Curtain	B	
King's #29	A	
King's #500	B	
Kitchen Stove, The	C	Also called Jersey
Klondike	F+	
Knight (U.S. Shell)	A	
Knobby Bull's-Eye	A	

Late Panelled Grape

Pattern	Key	
Lacy Cable	C	
Lacy Daisy	C	
Lacy Dewdrop	B	
Lacy Floral	B	
Lady Medallion	A	
Lacy Spiral	B	
Lacy Valance	A	
Ladders	A	
Ladder-to-the-Stars	A	
Ladder with Diamonds	A	Bud vase (See Egg Cup)
Lady Hamilton	C	
Lakewood	A	
Large Stippled Chain	B	
Late Block	B	Ruby-flashed — Key C
Late Butterfly	C	
Late Colonial	A	
Late Colonial Variant	A	
Late Crystal	A	
Late Diamond Point Band	A	
Late Panelled Grape	B	
Late Rosette	A	
Late Sawtooth (Zipper)	B	
Late Swan	D	Opaque glass
Late Thistle	B	
Late Washington	A	No decoration
Latin Cross	B	
Lattice	A	

Pattern	Key
Lattice & Lens	A
Leaf & Dart	C
Leaf & Flower	C
Leaf & Rib	A
Leaf & Star	A
Leaf Bracket	C
Leaf in Oval	A
Leaf Medallion	A
Leaflets	A
Leaf Rosette	B
Leafy Scroll	B
Leaning Pillars	B
Lee	E
Lenox	A
Lens & Block	B
Lens & Star	B
Liberty	E
Liberty Bell	C
Lightning	B
Lily-of-the-Valley	C
Lincoln Drape	E
Lincoln Drape with Tassel	F
Lion	C
Lion & Baboon	D
Lion's Leg (Alaska)	E
Lippman	A
Little Balls	A
Little Band	A
Little Bullet	A
Little Daisy	B
Little Gem	B
Little Owl	D
Little River	B
Locket	A
Locket on Chain	C
Loehr Flute	B
Loganberry & Grape	B
Log & Star	B
Log Cabin	F
Long Buttress	B

Leaf and Star

.. with finial — Key C

.. Mug with snake &
pitcher are rare

.. Colored glass

D Miniature

B Pickle Jar, See Goblet

36

Loop with Elk

Louise

Man's Head

37

Pattern	Key	
Marquisette	C	
Marsh Fern	B	
Marsh Pink	C	
Mary Jane	A	
Maryland	A	
Mascotte	B	
Masonic	B	
Massachusetts	B	
Maypole	A	
McKee's Comet	A	
McKee's Stars & Stripes	A	
McKee's Sunburst	A	
McKee's Virginia	A	
Medallion	B	
Medallion Sprig	A	
Medallion Sunburst	B	
Mellor	B	
Melrose	B	Tray, See Creamer
Melton	C	
Memphis	C	
Mephistopheles	D	Ale glass, See tumbler price
Merrimac	A	
Michigan	B	
Midget Thumbprint	C	
Midwestern Hairpin	F	
Millard	B	
Milton	A	
Minerva	D	
Minnesota	B	
Minor Block	B	
Mioton	A	
Mioton-Pleat Band	B	
Mirror	C	Flint price
Mirror, The	A	
Mirror & Loop	B	
Mirror (Kamm's)	A	
Mirror Star	B	
Miss America	A	"Depression Glass"
Missouri	A	
Mitre Cut	A	"Depression Glass"

Marsh Fern

Michigan

Pattern	Key
Mitred Diamond	A
Mitred Prisms	A
Model Peerless	A
Moesser	A
Monkey	E
Monkey Under Tree	F
Monroe	E
Moon & Star	C
Moon & Stork	D
Morning Glory	B
Mosaic, The	B
Mosaic Scroll	A
Mt. Vernon	D
Multiple Circle	A
Multiple Scroll	B
Murano	B

Mitred Diamond

Nail	C
Nail City	A
Nailhead	A
Narcissus Spray	A
Narrow Swirl	A
National's Eureka	A
National #681	B
Near Cut	A
Near Cut #2651	B
Nelly	B
Nestor	A
Net & Scroll	B
Netted Oak	B
Netted Ribbons	C . . Milk Glass
Nevada	A
New England Pineapple	D
New Era	A
New Hampshire	B
New Jersey	C
Niagara	A
Nickel Plate #26	B
Nickel Plate's Richmond	A

Near Cut

Niagara

Northwood Peach

Ohio (Etched)

Pattern	Key
Ovals & Fine Pleat	B
Oval Star	A
Oval Thumbprint	A
Oval Thumbprint Band	C
Oval Windows	A
Overall Lattice	A
Ovoid Panels	A
Owl & Possum	E
Owl, Milk Glass	C
Owl & Fan (Parrot)	C
Paddlewheel	A
Paddlewheel Shield	A
Paisley	B
Paling	A
Palm Beach	B
Palmer Prism	C
Palm Leaf	C . . Milk Glass
Palm Leaf Fan	B
Palmette	C
Pampas Flower	B
Panama	A
Panel & Cane	A
Panel & Flute	A
Panel & Rib	A
Panel with Diamond Point Band	A
Panel Rib Shell	B
Panelled Acorn Band	D
Panelled Anthemion	A
Panelled Beads	A
Panelled Cable	B
Panelled Cane	B
Panelled Cardinal	C
Panelled Cherry	B
Panelled Daisies — Fine Cut	B
Panelled Daisy	B
Panelled Dewdrop	B
Panelled Diamond & Flowers	B
Panelled Diamond Blocks	A

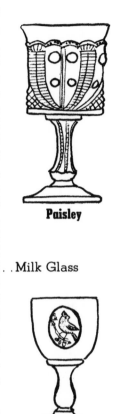

Paisley

Panelled Cardinal

Panelled Diamond & Flowers

41

Pattern	Key
Panelled Diamond Cross	A
Panelled Diamond Cut and Fan	A
Panelled Diamond Point	B
Panelled Diamonds & Rosettes	B
Panelled English Hobnail	B
Panelled Fern	C
Panelled Fine Cut	A
Panelled Finetooth	A
Panelled Flattened Sawtooth	A
Panelled Flower Stippled	C
Panelled Forget-Me-Not	C
Panelled 44	B
Panelled Grape	B
Panelled Grape Band	C
Panelled Heather	B
Panelled Hobnail	B
Panelled Holly	B
Panelled Holly & Diamond	A
Panelled Honeycomb	B
Panelled Ivy	B
Panelled Ladder	B
Panelled Lattice	A
Panelled Oak	B
Panelled Oval	C
Panelled Palm	A
Panelled Pleat	A
Panelled Primula	A
Panelled Rib	A
Panelled Ringed Stem	A
Panelled Roman Key	B
Panelled "S"	B
Panelled Sagebrush	B
Panelled Sawtooth	A
Panelled Smocking	A

Panelled Fern

Panelled Ivy

Pattern	Key
Panelled Sprig	B
Panelled Star & Button	B
Panelled Strawberry	A
Panelled Strawberry Cut	B
Panelled Sunflower	A
Panelled Swan	C
Panelled Thistle	C . . Bee-mark Toothpick Key D
Panelled Thousand Eye	C
Panelled Thumbprint	A
Panelled Wheat	A
Pannier	B
Pansy	A
Pansy & Moss Rose	B
Pantagraph Band	B
Parachute	B
Parian Swirl	B
Paris	A
Parrot	C
Pathfinder	B
Patricia	B
Pattee Cross	B
Pavonia	B
Pecan Swirl	B
Peacock & Palm	A
Peacock at the Fountain*	D
Peacock Feather	B
Pebbled Swirl	B
Peerless	C
Pendant	A
Pennsylvania	B
Pentagon	B
Pequot	C
Periwinkle	A
Persian	A
Petal & Loop	C
Petticoat	B
Philadelphia	B
Phytolacca	A
Picket	B
Picket Band	B
Picture Window	A

Pantagraph Band

Pattee Cross (Georgia)

43

*Carnival Glass

Pattern	Key	
Pigs in Corn	D	Goblet only known
Pilgrim Bottle	C	
Pillar	C	
Pillar Bull's-Eye	C	
Pillow & Sunburst	B	
Pillow Bands	A	
Pillow Encircled	A	
Pillow in Oval	B	
Pillows	C	
Pimlico	A	
Pineapple	A	
Pineapple & Fan	A	
Pineapple & Fan (Heisey's)	B	
Pinwheel	A	
Pioneer #15	A	
Pioneer #21	A	
Pioneer's Victoria	B	
Pittman	A	
Pittsburgh Fan	B	
Pittsburgh Flute	B	
Plaid	C	
Plain Roman Key	D	
Plain Scalloped Panel	A	
Plain Tulip	C	
Plain Two-Mold	A	
Pleat & Panel	B	
Pleat Band	A	
Pleated Bands	A	
Pleated Medallion	C	
Pleated Oval	A	
Pleating	D	
Plume	B	
Plutec	A	
Plytec	B	
Pogo Stick	A	
Pointed Arches	A	
Pointed Gothic	A	
Pointed Jewel	B	
Polar Bear	F	
Popcorn	C	

Pillar

Plume

44

Pattern	Key	
Pond Lily	C	
Portland Petal	C	
Portland	C	
Post Script	A	
Potted Plant (Flowerpot)	C	
Powder & Shot	C	Flint — Key D
Pressed Block	E	
Pressed Diamond	B	
Pressed Leaf	B	Flint — Key D
Pressed Leaf with Chain	A	
Pressed Octagon	A	
Pressed Spray	B	
Pressed Swirl	B	
Pretty Panels	A	
Primrose	B	
Primrose & Pearls	B	
Prince of Wales Plumes	C	
Princess Feather	C	
Princess Hobnail	B	
Priscilla	C	
Priscilla — Fostoria's	B	
Prism	C	
Prism & Crescent	C	
Prism & Diamond	B	
Prism & Herringbone	A	
Prism & Flattened Sawtooth	C	
Prism & Flute	A	
Prism & Herringbone	A	
Prism & Sawtooth	C	
Prismatic	A	
Prism-Bakewell's	A	
Prism Bars	A	
Prism Buttress (Cordova)	B	
Prism Column	A	
Prism Cube	B	
Prism with Ball and Buttons	B	
Prism with Diamond Points	B	

Pond Lily

Pattern	Key
Prism with Double Block Band	B
Prison Window	A
Prize, The	B
Pseudo-Czarina	A
Psyche & Cupid	D
Puffed Bands	A
Punty Bands	B
Punty & Diamond Point	B
Pyramids	A

Punty Band

Quadruped	B
Quartered Block One	B
Quartered Block Two	C
Quatrefoil	A
Queen	A
Queen Anne	C
Queen's Jewels	B
Question Mark	B
Quilt & Flute	A
Quilted Fan Top	A
Quilted Phlox	B
Quintec	A

..Pitcher — Key E

Rabbit in Tree	B
Racing Deer	D
Radiant	B
Rainbow	A
Rainbow Variant	A
Raindrop	A
Raspberry	B
Ray	B
Ray-McKee's	B
Rayed Flower	A
Rayed with Loop	A
Rebecca at the Well	F
Recessed Pillar	B
Red Flute	C

Racing Deer

..Colored Glass

Pattern	Key	
Red Sunflower	B	Clear
Reeding	A	
Regal	A	
Regal Block	A	
Regina	A	
Reticulated Cord	B	
Reward	A	
Rex	A	
Rexford (Euclid)	A	
Rib & Bead	B	
Rib & Block	A	
Rib & Swirl	C	Milk Glass
Rib Band	A	
Ribbed Acorn	C	
Ribbed Bands	B	
Ribbed Forget-Me-Not	A	
Ribbed Grape	C	Flint — Key D
Ribbed Palm	C	
Ribbed Thumbprint	B	
Ribbed Ware	A	
Ribbing	C	
Ribbon	B	Dolphin compote-Key E
Ribs & Diamonds	A	
Ribs over Ribs	C	
Richards & Hartley's #900	B	
Richmond	B	
Ridge Swirl	A	
Right Swirl	B	
Ring & Block	B	
Ring & Swirl	B	
Ring-Handled Basket	B	
Ripple	A	
Rising Sun	B	
Riverside	A	
Riverside's Victoria	B	
Roanoke	B	
Roanoke Star	A	
Robin Hood	B	
Rock Crystal	A	

Ribbed Grape

Pattern	Key	
Rocket	B	
Rocket Bomb	B	Gilded
Rococo	C	
Roman	B	
Roman Key	C	
Roman Key, Frosted Band	C	
Roman Key Base	B	
Roman Key Collar	B	
Roman Rosette	C	
Rope & Ribs	A	
Rope & Thumbprint	B	
Rope Bands	B	
Rope Panel	A	
Roped Diamond	C	
Rose in Snow	C	
Rosepoint Band	A	
Rose Sprig	B	
Rosette	C	
Rosette & Palms	B	
Rosette Row	B	
Rosette with Pinwheels	A	
Rose Windows	C	
Rose Wreath	A	
Rotec	A	
Royal	A	
Royal Ivy	D	Colored F+
Royal Oak	D	Colored F+
Ruby	B	Clear
Ruby Diamond	B	Clear
Ruby Rosette	D	Ruby-Stained
Ruffled Eye	E	Colored glass
Ruffles	A	
Saloon	A	
Sandwich Flute (Flute)	B	
Sandwich Loop	C	
Sandwich Plaid	E	
Sandwich Star	C	Goblet 4 X Key E

Roman Rosette

48

Pattern	Key
Sandwich Star & Buckle	F+
Sawtooth	C .. Non-flint — Key B
Sawtooth & Star	A
Sawtooth & Window	A
Sawtooth Bottom	A
Sawtoothed Honeycomb	B
Saxon	B
Scallop Shell	A
Scalloped Flower Band	C
Scalloped Lines	B
Scalloped Swirl	C
Scalloped Tape	A .. Tray, See Celery -Key C

Scroll & Flower Stars

Pattern	Key
Screen	A
Scroll	A
Scroll & Chain	B
Scroll & Daisy	A .. Carnival — Key C
Scroll Band	A
Scroll & Flower Stars	B
Scroll & Flower Swirl	B
Scroll in Scroll	A
Scroll with Acanthus	A
Scroll with Cane Band	D
Scroll with Flowers	B
Scroll with Star	B
Scrolled Spray	C .. Milk Glass
Scrolled Sunflower	A
Seashell	A
Sectional Block	A
Seed Pod	B
Seely	A
Semi-Oval	B
Sequoia	A
Serrated Prism, Banded	A
Serrated Rib	B
Serrated Rib & Fine Cut	A
Serrated Spearpoint	A
Sharp Oval & Diamond	A
Sheaf & Block	B
Shell, U.S.	A
Shell & Jewel	A
Shell & Scale	B

Scroll & Flower Swirl

49

Pattern	Key	
Shell & Tassel	B	
Shelton Star	A	
Shepherds Plaid	A	
Sheraton	A	Bread plate, See pitcher
Shield	B	
Shield & Spike	B	
Shimmering Star	B	
Shrine	C	
Shoshone	B	
Shuttle	B	
Side Wheeler	B	
Silver Queen	B	
Singing Birds	C	
Single Rose	B	
Siskyou	A	
Sister Kate	A	
Sisters, The (Three Face)	E	
Six Panel Fine Cut	B	
Six Pansy	B	
Skilton	B	
Slashed Swirl	B	
Slewed Diamond	B	
Slewed Horseshoe	B	Syrup Key C
Slipper	Shoe — See Celery Key C	
Smocking	E	
Smooth Diamond	B	
Snail	D	
Snakeskin	B	
Snakeskin with Dot	B	
Snowflake	B	
Snowflake & Sunburst	B	
Snowflake Base	A	
Snowshoe	B	
Southern Ivy	A	
Spanish American	D	Tumbler — Key E
Spearheads	B	
Spearpoint Band	B	
Specialty	A	
Specialty's Pattern E	A	
Spiral & Maltese Cross	B	
Spiralled Diamond Point	C	

Shoshone

Snail (Idaho)

Pattern	Key
Spiralled Ivy	B
Spiralled Triangle	A
Spirea Band	B
Spotted Box	C
Sprig	C . . Wine — Key D
Sprig in Snow	B
Sprig without Sprig	A
Square Block	A
Square Flute	B
Squared Daisy & Diamond	B
Squared Fine Cut	B
Squared Star	A
Squared Sunburst	B
Squat Pineapple	B
Squirrel	D
Squirrel-in-Bower	D
Squirrel with Nut	D
S-Repeat	B
Staple	A
Star	B
Star & Bar	B
Star & Circle	B
Star & Diamond	B
Star & Diamond Point	B
Star & Fan	A
Star & Feather	B
Star & Feather, Lee's	C
Star & Ladders	B
Star & Notched Rib	B
Star & Palm	B
Star & Punty	2 X F
Star & Rib	B
Star & Swag	D
Star & Thumbprint	E
Star Band	A
Star & Diamondpoint	B
Star Base	A
Stardust	A
Star in Bull's-Eye	B

Star

Star & Circle

Pattern	Key
Star in Diamond	A
Star in Honeycomb	B
Star in Octagon	A
Star in Pillar	B
Star in Square	B
Starlyte	A
Star Medallion	B
Star of Bethlehem	A
Star of David	A
Star Octad	A
Star Pattern	C
Star Rosetted	B
Starred Block	B
Starred Cosmos	A
Starred Loop	B
Starred Scroll	B
Stars & Bars	B
Stars & Bars with Leaf	C
Stars & Stripes	A
Star with Zippers	A
States, The	B
St. Bernard	D
Stedman	C
Stepped Diamond Point	E
Sterling	B
Stippled Acanthus	B
Stippled Band	B
Stippled Bar	C
Stippled Chain	C
Stippled Cherry	B
Stippled Clover	C
Stippled Dahlia	C
Stippled Daisy	B
Stippled Dart & Balls	A
Stippled Diamond Band	C
Stippled Flower Band	A
Stippled Forget-Me-Not	B
Stippled Grape & Festoon	B
Stippled Ivy	C

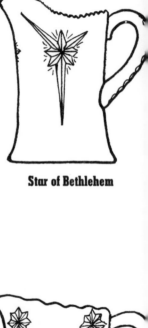

Star of Bethlehem

Sterling

Pattern	Key
Stippled Leaf	B
Stippled Leaf, Flower and Moth	D
Stippled Loop	A
Stippled Loop with Vine Band	B
Stippled Medallion	C
Stippled Palm	C
Stippled Panel & Band	C
Stippled Sandbur	A
Stippled Star	A
Stippled Star Flower	A
Stippled Strawberry	B
Stippled Woodflower	B
Stratford	A
Strawberry	C
Strawberry & Currant	B
Strawberry & Fan Variant	D
Strawberry & Fan Variant Two	B
Strawberry with Checkerboard	B
Strigil	B
Strutting Peacock	C
Style	B
Summit, The	B
Sunbeam	B
Sunburst	A
Sunburst & Bar	B
Sunburst & Star	A
Sunburst-Diamond	B
Sunburst on Shield	A
Sunflower	B
Sunk Daisy	B
Sunk Diamond & Lattice	A
Sunk Honeycomb	B
Sunk Jewel	B
Sunk Prism	D
Sunken Arches	A

Stippled Leaf

. . Milk Glass — Key F

The Summit

Pattern	Key
Tarantum Thumbprint	A
Tassel & Bead	A
Teardrop	A
Teardrop & Diamond Block (Art)	C
Teardrop & Tassel	C
Teardrop Flower	A
Teardrop Row	A
Teasel	B
Tennis Racquet	B
Ten-Pointed Star	B
Tepee	B
Teutonic	A
Texas	B
Texas Bull's-Eye	B
Texas Star	B
Thimble	C
Thistle	C
Thistle & Clover	A
Thistle & Fern	B
Thistleblow	B
Thousand Diamonds	A
Thousand Eye	C
Thread Band	A
Threading	A
Three Deer	D
Three Face	E
Three-in-One	A
Three Leaf Clover	D
Three Panel	B
Three-Ply Panel	A
Thrush	C
Thrush & Apply Blossoms	C
Thumbprint & Diamond	A
Thumbprint Block	B
Thumbprint on Spearpoint	A
Thumbprint Row	A
Thumbprint Windows	C
Tieback	B
Tidy	A

Thistle

Egg Cup — Key D

Texas

Pattern	Key	
Tile	B	
Tiny Lion	B	
Tiptoe	A	
Tokyo	B	
Toltec	A	
Tong	D	Flint
Toothed Medallion	B	
Top & Bottom Scroll	A	
Torpedo	B	
Tossed Scrolls	B	
Town Pump, The	D	
Transverse Ribs	A	
Tree Bark	A	
Tree of Life	C	
Tree of Life with Hand	E	
Tree of Life with Sprig	A	
Trellis Scroll	A	
Tremont	A	
Triad	A	
Triangular Medallion	B	
Triangular Prism	D	
Triple Band	B	
Triple Bead Band	A	
Triple Bar	B	
Triple Bar & Loop	A	
Trible Bar with Cable	B	
Triple Fine Tooth Band	A	
Triple Frosted Band	B	
Triple Line	B	
Triple Prism-Grid	A	
Triple Shell	C	
Triple Thumbprints	A	
Triple Triangle	B	
Triple X	A	
Truncated Cone	A	
Truncated Cube	A	
Tulip	E	Flint
Tulip Band	C	
Tulip Petals	C	

Tong

Tulip

Twin Snowshoes

Unique

**Twinkle Star
(Utah)**

Pattern	Key
Valentine	C
Venice	A
Vermont	D*
Vesta	B
V-Band	A
Victoria	E
Victorian Jubilee	A
Vigilant	A
Vine	D
V-in-Heart	B
Virginia	B
Vulcan	A

Vesta

Wading Heron	D
Waffle	D . . Flint
Waffle & Bar	B
Waffle & Fine Cut	B
Waffle & Star Band	A
Waffle & Thumbprint	D . . Water Pitcher — Key F
Waffle Keg	C
Waffle Octagon	B
Waffle Window	A
Waffle With Points	A
Ward's New Era	A
Washboard	B
Washington Centennial	D
Washington Early	E
Washington Late	E . . Flashed & Painted
Waterfall	B
Waterlily & Cattails	B
Wave	A
Waverly	B
Wavey	B
Wedding Bells	A
Wedding Ring	B
Wellington	A
Weston	A
Westmoreland	B
Westward Ho!	F
Wheat & Barley	A
Wheel & Comma	C

Wedding Ring

*See *PATTERN GLASS PRIMER*, Plate 284

Pattern	Key

Wild Rose with Bow-Knot — Key B

Wigwam

Pattern	Key
Zenith	B
Zenith Block	A
Zephyr	B
Zig-Zag	B
Zig-Zag Band	B
Zig-Zag Block	A
Zipper	B
Zipper Slash	B
Zipper Borders	A
Zippered Block	A
Zippered Diamond	A

Zipper

Alternate Names For Patterns

-A-

Acme — See Butterfly with Spray
Acorn — See Netted Oak
Acorn — See Willow Oak
Adams — See King's #29
Adams Crystal Wedding — See Box Pleat
Admiral Dewey — See Spanish American
Adonis — See Washboard
Alaric — See Butterfly Ears
Alaska — See Klondike
Alaska — See Lion's Leg
Alexis — See Priscilla
Amberette — See Klondike
American — See Swirl & Diamond
American — See Zig-Zag Block
Andes — See Beaded Tulip
Annie — See Actress
Apple Blossom — See Art Nouveau
Arctic — See Polar Bear
Artichoke — See Valencia
Ashman — See Etched Fern
Athenia — See Panelled 44
Atlanta — See Clear Lion's Head
Atlanta — See Lion
Austrian — See Fine Cut Medallion
Aztec Sunburst — See McKee's Sunburst

-B-

Baby Thumbprint — See Dakota
Balder — See Pensylvania
Balky Mule — See Currier & Ives
Barred Block — See Late Block
Barrelled Block — See Late Block
Beaded Jewel — See Lacy Dewdrop
Beaded Mirror — See Beaded Medallion
Beaded Oval & Leaf — See Jewel & Flower
Beaded Ovals — See Beaded Loops
Beaded Yoke — See Bead Swag
Bean — See Egg in Sand
Bearded Man — See Queen Anne
Bent Buckle — See New Hampshire
Berkeley — See Blocked Arches
Bessimer Flute — See Flute
Big Block — See Henrietta
Blackberry & Grape — See Loganberry & Grape
Blazing Pinwheels — See Shoshone
Block — See Belmont's Reflecting Fans
Blockade — See Diamond Block with Fan
Block & Star — See Valencia Waffle
Block Barrel — See Greensburg's #130
Block Midriff — See Regal

Bosworth — See Star Band
Boylan — See Euclid
Bradford Blackberry — See Bradford Grape
Brazil — See Panelled Daisy
Brazilian — See Cane Shield
Brilliant — See Stars & Stripes
Broughton — See Pattee Cross
Bullet — See Cannonball
Bull's-Eye — See Wyoming
Bull's Eye in Heart — See Heart with Thumbprint

-C-

Cameo — See Ceres; Also see Classic Medallion
Canadian Drape — See Garfield Drape
Candy Ribbon — See Bryce
Cane & Star Medallion — See The States
Chain with Diamonds — See Washington Centennial
Champion — See Diamond & Long Sunburst
Chickenwire — See Sawtoothed Honeycomb
Chrysanthemum Leaf — See Curled Leaf
Clematis — See Rose Point Band
Coin Spot — See Inverted Thumbprint
Colonial — See Jefferson #270
Comet — See Horn of Plenty
Cordate Leaf — See Homestead
Corona — See Sunk Honeycomb
Crane — See Clear Stork
Crescent — See Fringed Drape
Crown & Shield — See Persian
Crown Jewels — See Chandelier; or Queen's Jewels
Crowfoot — See Yale
Crystal Ball — See Atlas; or Eyewinker
Cube & Diamond — See Milton
Cubist — See Cube, L. T.

-D-

Daisies in Oval Panels — See Bull's Eye and Fan
Daisy & Bluebell — See Mosaic, The
Daisy & Cube — See Stars and Bars
Daisy and Cube with Oval Panels — See Hartley
Darby — See Pleat & Panel
Deer & Doe — See Deer & Pine Tree
Derby — See Pleat and Panel
Dewdrop & Fan — See Beaded Fan
Dewey — See Flower Flange; or Spanish American
Diamond & Teardrop — See Tarantum's Atlanta

61

Diamond Block & Fan — See Pineapple
& Fan
Diamond Medallion — See Grand
Diamonds in Oval — See X-Logs
Dinner Bell — See Cottage
Divided Squares — See Hobb's Block
Dogwood — See Art Nouveau
Doll's Eye — See Memphis
Doric — See Feather; or Indiana
Dot — See Beaded Oval & Scroll
Double Arch — See also Empress
Double Flute — See Ashburton
Double Loop — See Bryce
Double Prism — See Heck
Double Red Block — See Hexagon Bull's
Eye
Draped Fan — See U.S. Comet
Draped Red Block — See Loop & Block
Draped Red Top — See Riverside's
Victoria
Draped Top — See Riverside's Victoria
Duchess Flute — See Flute
Dutchess Loop — See Flute

-E-

Egg & Dart — See Hourglass
Eighteen Ninety — See Block & Palm
Emerald Green Herringbone — See
Green Herringbone
English Hobnail Cross — See Klondike
English Hobnail Variant — See Sylvan
Enigma — See Wyoming
Esther — See Prism with Double Block
Band
Etched Dakota — See Dakota
Etched Fern & Waffle — See Mascotte
Excelsior with Double Ringed Stem —
See Hourglass
Excelsior — See Giant Bull's Eye

-F-

Fairfax Strawberry — See Strawberry
Fan & Flute — See Millard
Fan with Acanthus Leaf — See Long Fan
with Acanthus Leaf
Fig — See Baltimore Pear
Figure Eight — See Bryce
Filley — See Texas Bull's Eye
Fine Cut & Feather — See Feather
Fine Cut & Ribbed Bars — See Taran-
tum's Ladder with Diamond
Fine Cut Band — See Cottage
Fine Cut Bar — See Panama
Fish-Eye — See Torpedo
Flag — See Centennial Shield
Flambeau — See Prince of Wales Plumes
Flamingo — See Frosted Stork
Flat Diamond — See Diamond Quilted
Imperial

Flora — See also Opposing Pyramids
Flower Spray with Scrolls — See Intaglio
Flying Robin — See Hummingbird
Francesware Swirl — See Blown Swirl
Frost Flower — See Twinkle Star
Frosted Chain — See Chain with Star
Frosted Waffle — See Hidalgo

-G-

Gem — See Late Block
Georgia Gem — See Little Gem
Gipsy — See Baltimore Pear
Gloved Hand — See Coat-of-Arms
Good Luck — See Horseshoe
Grecian Swirl — See Cyclone

-H-

Hanover — See Block with Stars
Hearts & Spades — See Medallion
Hearts of Loch Laven - See Shuttle
Heisey's Plantation — See Florida
Pineapple
Herringbone Band — See Ripple
Hexagon Block — See Hexagon
Bull's-Eye
Hexagonal Block — See Valencia Waffle
Himoto — See Diamond Point with
Panels
Holbrook — See Pineapple & Fan
Hops & Barley — See Wheat and Barley
Huckle — See Feather Duster

-I-

Ida — See Sheraton
Idaho — See Snail
Indiana Swirl — See Feather
Interlocking Crescents — See Double
Arch
Inverness — See Oval Thumbprint
Inverted Loops & Fan — See Maryland
Inverted Thistle — See Late Thistle
Ionic — See Arabian
Iowa — See Zippered Block
Ivorina Verde — See Winged Scroll

-J-

Jewel & Crescent — See Jewelled Rosettes
Job's Tears — See Art

-K-

Kamoni — See Pennsylvania
Kansas — See Jewel with Dewdrop
Kirkland — See Sunk Daisy

-L-

Lace — See Drapery
Late Buckle — See Buckle with Star
Late Icicle — See Belted Icicle

63

Red Block — See Late Block
Red Block & Lattice — See Button & Star
Red Top — See Button Arches
Reeded Waffle — See Berlin
Reed Stem Flute — See Flute
Reflecting Fans — See Belmont's Reflecting Fans
Reverse Torpedo — See Bull's-eye Band
Rexford — See Euclid
Rhode Island — See Fine Ribbed Anchor & Shield
Ribbed Ellipse — See Admiral
Ribbed Ivy — See Ivy
Ribbed Pineapple — See Prism & Flattened Sawtooth
Rochelle — See Princess Feather
Roman Cross — See Crossed Block
Romeo — See Block & Fan
Rope — See Colonial, Fluted
Royal Crystal — See Tarantum's Atlanta
Ruby Thumbprint — See King's Crown

·S·

Sanborn — See Iron Kettle
Sandwich Flute — See Flute
Sawtooth Band — See Amazon
Scalloped Band — See Scalloped Lines
Scalloped Diamond Point - See Late Diamond Point Band
Scalloped Loop — See Yoked Loop
Sedan — See Panelled Star & Button
Shell & Scroll — See Geneva
Smocking Bands — See Double Beetle Band
Spades — See Medallion
Square Fuscia — See Marsh Pink
Star & Oval — See Lens & Star
Star Base Swirl — See Texas Star
Star Flower Band — See Stippled Flower Band
Starred Jewel — See Louise
Stemless Daisy — See Cosmos
Stepped Arch Panel — See Chippendale
Stippled Beaded Shield — See Locket on Chain
Stippled Scroll — See Scroll
Stippled Star — See Willow Oak
Stippled Violet — See Dewdrop & Flowers
Stork — See Clear Stork
Stork Looking at the Moon — See Moon & Stork
Stylistic Leaf — See Medallion Sprig
Stylized Flower — See Flower & Panel
Sun & Star — See Priscilla
Sunburst Medallion — See Daisy Medallion

Sunburst Rosette — See Frosted Medallion
Sunk — See Queen
Sunken Primrose — See Florida
Sunrise — See Rising Sun
Sweet Pear — See Avocado
Swirl & Star — See Texas Star
Swirled Block — See Westmoreland

·T·

Tapered Vine — See Aster & Leaf
Teardrop & Diamond Block — See Art
Tennessee — See Jewelled Rosettes
Texas Swirl — See Texas Star
Three-Faced Medallion — See Actress Chain
Three Graces — See Three Face
Three Stories — See Persian
Thumbprint — See Argus
Thumbprint Band — See Dakota
Tidal — See Florida Palm
Tripod Stem — See Arched Tripod
Truncated Prisms — See Opposing Pyramids
Tulip with Sawtooth — See Tulip
Turtle — See Garden of Eden
Twin Pear — See Baltimore Pear

·V·

Vermont — See Honeycomb with Flower Rim
Vernon — See Honeycomb
Victor — See Shoshone; Also Shell & Jewel
Viking — See Bearded Head; Also Panama

·W·

Waterlily — See Magnolia; Also Rose Point Band
Wheat — See Panelled Wheat
Wigwam — See Tepee
Wild Rose — See Art Nouveau
Wisconsin — See Beaded Dewdrop
Wycliff — See Scroll With Star

64